My World
Toys & Games

GW01402617

* Especially suited for early years

© 2011 Out of the Ark Ltd

Introduction

The *My World* series of books is a fantastic collection of topic-based songbooks. Each includes twelve easy-to-learn and catchy songs by some of Britain's most popular children's songwriters. The accompanying CD features all songs sung by children along with professionally produced backing tracks.

Developed specifically for young children, we feel that the music and topics covered in this *Toys & Games* collection are particularly appropriate for use with children up to the age of around six. The songs can be used to supplement the 'creative' requirements of the foundation stage, as well as contributing to many other areas of the curriculum. Each lyric page contains helpful teacher's notes to expand and develop the subject content of the songs.

In addition to the teaching ideas given with each song, we suggest adding some simple percussion using instruments available in the classroom, and perhaps some homemade ones. It's important that children relate to music as something that they can become actively involved with and enjoy. Using percussion and easy clapping rhythms gives everyone a chance to really join in.

I Wish I Had A Robot

Words and Music by Mary Green and Julie Stanley

1. I wish I had a robot to tie up my laces,
   I wish I had a robot to tidy up my toys.
   I wish I had a robot to hang up my coat and
   I wish I had a robot with a robot voice.

   CHORUS   *Yes Sir, no Sir, let me have a go Sir,*
   Yes Sir, no Sir, I do what you say.
   Yes Sir, no Sir, let me have a go Sir,
   Yes Sir, no Sir, you go out to play.

2. I wish I had a robot to carry my school bag,
   I wish I had a robot to show to all the boys.
   I wish I had a robot to finish my homework,
   I wish I had a robot with a robot voice.

   CHORUS

- Pair the children up so that one of them is the robot and one of them is the child. Get the child to give the robot simple instructions and see if the robot can follow them, and then let the children swap roles.

- If the children had a robot, what sorts of things would they want the robot to do for them?

- Encourage the children to think of other toys that follow instructions or signals.

The Park

Words and Music by Paul Field

CHORUS   *Round and round the roundabout,*
Up and down the slide,
Swinging on the swings we go,
So high, so high.
We can climb the climbing frame,
Or see-saw to and fro,
How we love to go
To the park.

1. Running, jumping, bouncing, bumping,
There is so much space.
If you come it's so much fun,
There is no better place.

CHORUS

2. Hopping, skipping, sliding, slipping,
No one minds the noise.
Making friends and playing games,
There's so much to enjoy.

CHORUS   *Round and round the roundabout,*
Up and down the slide,
Swinging on the swings we go,
So high, so high.
We can climb the climbing frame,
Or see-saw to and fro,
How we love to go, how we love to go,
How we love to go to the park.

- This is a great song for actions. Split the class into groups and assign each group one of the activities from the chorus. Listening carefully to the song, see if the groups can do their action at the correct time during the choruses.

Old Toys, New Toys

Words and Music by Mary Green and Julie Stanley

CHORUS   *Old toys, new toys, made for us to play with,*
Old toys, new toys, let's have fun!
Old toys, new toys, everyone can share them,
Old toys, new toys, let's have fun!

1. Gran's old teddy bear is stuffed with sawdust,
   Grandpa's aeroplane is made of wood.
   Dad's old pedal car is scratched and rusty,
   Mum's old spinning top is not much good.

   CHORUS

2. Gran sneaks off to ride my shiny scooter,
   Grandpa likes to play computer games.
   Dad gives orders to my talking robot,
   Mum goes rollerblading down the lane!

   CHORUS

- How can we find out about old toys?

- Talk about the differences between the toys that the children's grandparents and parents played with and the toys the children have today. What materials are the old toys made out of and what materials are most of the children's toys made out of today?

- Do the children play with any of the same toys that their parents or grandparents played with? If so, how have they changed over the years?

- See if the children have seen or played with all the toys mentioned in the song.

I've Got A Cardboard Box

Words and Music by Mark and Helen Johnson

CHORUS   *I've got a cardboard box,*
A great big cardboard box,
It's plain and brown and empty
And it's had some knocks.
I've got a cardboard box,
A great big cardboard box,
It's nothing much to look at
But I like it such a lot!

1   It's... a... supersonic rocket, and I'm flying to the moon,
Hold tight, lean back, get there soon!
With my imagination there's no limit to the fun,
Supersonic rocket, my adventure's just begun.

CHORUS

2   It's... a... super-techno robot, and I'm clever as can be,
Hold tight, here comes mighty me!
With my imagination there's no limit to the fun,
Super-techno robot, my adventure's just begun.

CHORUS

3   It's... a... super-scary monster and I'm riding very high,
Hold tight, shout my battle-cry!
With my imagination there's no limit to the fun,
Super-scary monster, my adventure's just begun.
Super-scary monster, my adventure's just begun.

- Divide the class into six or nine groups, giving each group a card picturing the rocket, the robot or the monster from the song. Hand out a variety of percussion instruments for each group and get them to come up with sounds to depict what's on their card. Can the others guess what they are?

- Try making a rocket, a robot or a super-scary monster out of cardboard boxes. What sort of shapes would you need to make it?

Ready or Not

Words and Music by Matthew Crossey

(spoken) 1, 2, 3, 4, 5, 6, 7, 8, 9, 10.

CHORUS *Ready or not I'm coming,*
Ready or not here I come.
I'm counting to ten,
I hope you've hidden by then
'Cause ready or not here I come.

1. Are you under the stairs? NO!
Are you next to the chairs?
Are you there by the door? NO!
Are you crouched on the floor?

CHORUS

2. Are you under the bed? NO!
Is there a coat on your head?
Are you as quiet as can be? NO!
Are you somewhere near me?

CHORUS *Ready or not I'm coming,*
Ready or not here I come.
I'm counting to ten,
I hope you've hidden by then
'Cause ready or not here I come.
I'm counting to ten,
I hope you've hidden by then
'Cause ready or not here I come.

(spoken) I'VE FOUND YOU!

- Talk about whether the children like to play Hide and Seek. Do they like to do the looking or the hiding? Is Hide and Seek a new game or an old game? How can you find out?
- Find out about variations of the game Hide and Seek (e.g. Sardines).

I Love My Car The Best

Words and Music by Nikki Lewis

1. I love my car the best,
    It's faster than the rest,
    It's red and black with shiny wheels,
    I love my car the best.
    Beep, beep, beep, beep,
    Beep, beep, beep, beep.

2. I love my train the best,
    It's longer than the rest,
    Around and round the track it goes,
    I love my train the best.
    Choo, choo, choo, choo,
    Choo, choo, choo, choo.

3. I love my truck the best,
    It's stronger than the rest,
    It picks things up and puts them down,
    I love my truck the best.
    Vroom, vroom, vroom, vroom,
    Vroom, vroom, vroom, vroom.

4. I love my plane the best,
    It's louder than the rest,
    It swoops and glides across the sky,
    I love my plane the best.
    Zoom, zoom, zoom, zoom,
    Zoom, zoom, zoom, zoom.

- This song is full of exciting sounds that the children will enjoy singing. Can they think of other vehicles and the particular sounds that they make?

- Can the children find percussion instruments that make similar sounds to those in the song? Or perhaps they could think of a way of making an instrument to represent a particular vehicle (e.g. uncooked rice in a container for the 'choo choo' of the train).

- Encourage the children to use their instruments during the song, listening carefully to when their instrument should be played and trying to play in time to the music.

Building Bricks

Words and Music by Niki Davies

1. One brick, two bricks, steady as you go.
   Three bricks, four bricks, nice and slow.
   Five bricks, six bricks,
   I think it's getting wobbly,
   Is it going to topple down?

2. Seven bricks, eight bricks, steady as you go.
   Nine bricks, ten bricks, nice and slow.
   Eleven bricks, twelve bricks,
   I think it's getting wobbly,
   Is it going to topple down?

3. Thirteen, fourteen, steady as you go.
   Fifteen, sixteen, nice and slow.
   Seventeen, eighteen,
   I think it's getting wobbly,
   Oh, it's all come tumbling down!

- Ask the children to find different-shaped 3D objects around the classroom and see who can build the highest tower. How many can you stack on top of each other before it comes tumbling down?

- What makes some shapes easier to build? Which shapes do not make good building material?

Mr Jack-In-A-Box

Words and Music by Mark and Helen Johnson

1. All day long I sit here waiting,
   Hoping you might pick me up.
   All day long I wish you'd find me,
   Find me soon, 'cause I'm gonna go POP!
   Wind up my handle...
   Try to be careful...
   How many turns before you wake me up?
   Wind up my handle...
   Try to be careful...
   How many turns before my little lid goes 'POP'?!
   Say 'hello', I'm pleased to meet you
   Mr Jack-in-a-Box!

2. All day long I sit here waiting,
   Hoping you might pick me up.
   All day long I wish you'd find me,
   Find me soon, 'cause I'm gonna go POP!
   Wind up my handle...
   Try to be careful...
   How many turns before you wake me up?
   Wind up my handle...
   Try to be careful...
   How many turns before my little lid goes 'POP'?!
   Say 'hello', I'm pleased to meet you
   Mr Jack-in-a-Box!
   Say 'hello', I'm pleased to meet you
   Mr Jack-in-a-Box!

- Ask the children how they think the Jack-in-a-box is feeling in this song. Do the children ever feel bored or lonely? Talk about the things that the children prefer to do on their own and the things they like doing with other people.

- Try sitting the children in a circle with their eyes closed. Tap one of them on the shoulder and get them to jump up and shout, 'I'm Mr Jack-in-a-box'. When they've sat back down, the children can open their eyes and guess who jumped up – a great activity for listening skills.

- Get the children to sit down for the beginning of the song and then guess when the Jack is going to pop out of his box – did they jump up at the right time?

Teddy-Bear Rock

Words and Music by Ali Dee

Nobody knows about my teddy,
Nobody knows what he can do.
He does the teddy-bear stretch,
He does the teddy-bear flop,
He does the teddy-bear jig,
He does the teddy-bear rock.
Do, do-be-do-wop, the teddy-bear rock,
Do, do-be-do-wop, the teddy-bear rock,
Do, do-be-do-wop, my very, very special teddy bear
Does the teddy-bear rock.
(Repeat)

Do, do-be-do-wop, the teddy-bear rock,
Do, do-be-do-wop, the teddy-bear rock,
Do, do-be-do-wop, my very, very special teddy bear
Does the teddy-bear rock.

- Ask the children whether they've got their own special teddy bear or soft toy. Who gave it to them? What makes it so special?

- Draw a teddy bear doing one of the actions in the song.

- Discuss the difference between the teddy bears the children's grandparents had and the teddy bears the children have today. Are they made from the same materials? What are they stuffed with? What is used for eyes, noses and mouths?

- Get the children to stretch, flop, jig and rock like the teddy bear in the song. Can they listen carefully and do the actions in the right places?

The Dressing-Up Box

Words and Music by Nikki Lewis

1. I want to be a princess with a silver crown,
   I want to be a princess with a velvet gown.
   I want to be a princess with pink and shiny shoes,
   I want to be a princess, a princess I will choose.
   Open the box, the dressing-up box,
   I wonder what I could be.
   Open the box, the dressing-up box,
   Be a princess just like me.

2. I want to be a pirate with a spotty scarf,
   I want to be a pirate with a yo-ho laugh.
   I want to be a pirate, a patch over my eye,
   I want to be a pirate, a pirate I will try.
   Open the box, the dressing-up box,
   I wonder what I could be.
   Open the box, the dressing-up box,
   Be a pirate just like me.

3. I want to be a dragon with sharp and shiny claws,
   I want to be a dragon with green and slimy jaws.
   I want to be a dragon with a scaly chest,
   I want to be a dragon, a dragon would be best.
   Open the box, the dressing-up box,
   I wonder what I could be.
   Open the box, the dressing-up box,
   Be a dragon just like me.

4. I want to be a fireman with some heavy boots,
   I want to be a fireman with a navy suit.
   I want to be a fireman and slide right down the pole,
   I want to be a fireman, a fireman is my goal.
   Open the box, the dressing-up box,
   I wonder what I could be.
   Open the box, the dressing-up box,
   Be a fireman just like me.

> • Get the children to choose one of the four dressing-up characters and ask them to write a short story about him/her using some of the descriptive language used in the song. Which percussion instruments could they use to sound like the character in their story?

Turning The Skipping Rope

Words and Music by Mary Green and Julie Stanley

1. Turning the skipping rope, 1, 2, 3,
    In jumps Thomas, jumps like a flea.
    Keep on jumping while we count,
    One! Two! Three! Four! Five! Six! Seven! Eight!
    Time's up Thomas, you're out.

2. Turning the skipping rope, 1, 2, 3,
    In jumps Emma, jumps like a flea.
    Keep on jumping while we count,
    One! Two! Three! Four! Five! Six! Seven! Eight!
    Time's up Emma, you're out.

    We have provided four verses on the backing track to give you the opportunity to use four children's names during the song.

- Invent different games using a skipping rope. Can the children write a set of simple instructions to go with the game they've invented?

- Ask the children if they can think of other games that involve counting.

- What other games do the children play in the playground?

- Can the children find out what their parents and grandparents played in their school playgrounds? Are any of the games similar?

- Investigate rope. Get the children to paint using rope or string and see how many different shapes and patterns they can create.

Put It Back!

Words and Music by Mark and Helen Johnson

If you put it down, pick it up, pick it up!
If you got it out, put it back!
If you made a mess, clear it up, clear it up!
If you got it out, put it back!
Don't make someone else do the dirty work,
Do what you can do.
See how quickly things can be sorted out
When we all do what we can, not leave it to a few.

(Repeat song twice)

If you put it down, pick it up, pick it up!
If you got it out, put it back!
If you made a mess, clear it up, clear it up!
If you got it out, put it back!
If you got it out, put it back!

- Get the children to discuss the importance of tidying up. Why does it matter if we leave things all over the floor? Why should we put things back in their proper places? Why shouldn't we leave it to other people?

- Talk about the importance of recycling. Bring in a mixture of items on a tray and ask the children if they can sort them into paper, plastic, tin and general waste.

I Wish I Had A Robot

Words and Music by
Mary Green and Julie Stanley

Precise and rhythmic ♩ = 110

Lyrics:

1. I wish I had a ro-bot to tie up my la-ces, I wish I had a ro-bot to ti-dy up my toys. I wish I had a ro-bot to hang up my coat and I wish I had a ro-bot with a

(2.) wish I had a ro-bot to car-ry my school bag, I wish I had a ro-bot to show to all the boys. I wish I had a ro-bot to fin-ish my home-work, I wish I had a ro-bot with a

always short

ro - bot voice.
ro - bot voice.

Yes Sir, no Sir,

let me have a go Sir, yes Sir, no Sir, I do what you say.

Yes Sir, no Sir, let me have a go Sir, yes Sir, no Sir,

1.
you go out to play.

2.
2. I you go out to play.

The Park

Words and Music by
Paul Field

With energy ♩ = 150

Round and round_ the round - a - bout,_

up and down the slide,___ swing-ing on_ the swings_

so high, so high.

We can climb the climb - ing frame, or see-saw to and fro,

how we love to go to the park.

To Coda ⊕

19

1. Run - ning, jump - ing, boun - cing, bump - ing, there is so ___ much space. ___
2. Hop - ping, skip - ping, sli - ding, slip - ping, no-one minds the noise. ___

___ If you come ___ it's so ___ much fun, ___ there is ___
___ Ma-king friends and play - ing games, there's

no bet - ter place.

so much to__ en - joy.__

CODA

how we love__ to go,__

how we love__ to go to the park.

21

Old Toys, New Toys

Words and Music by
Mary Green and Julie Stanley

Old toys, new toys, made for us to play with,

old toys, new toys, let's have fun!

Old toys, new toys,

ev-ery-one can share them, old toys, new toys, let's have fun!

1. Gran's old ted-dy bear is stuffed with saw-dust, Grand-pa's ae-ro-plane is
2. Gran sneaks off to ride my shi-ny scoo-ter, Grand-pa likes to play com-

made of wood. Dad's old pe-dal car is scratched and rust-y,
-pu-ter games. Dad gives or-ders to my talk-ing ro-bot,

Mum's old spin-ning top is not much good.
Mum goes rol-ler-bla-ding

down the lane!

let's have fun!

I've Got A Cardboard Box

Words and Music by
Mark and Helen Johnson

Moderately ♩ = 104

I've got a card-board box, a
great big card-board box, it's plain and brown and emp-ty and it's
had some knocks. I've got a card-board box, a great big card-board box, it's

no - thing much to look at but I like it such a lot!

Slightly faster

1. It's a su - per - son - ic roc - ket, and I'm fly - ing to the moon,
2. It's a su - per - tech - no ro - bot, and I'm clev - er as can be,
3. It's a su - per - sca - ry mon - ster and I'm ri - ding ve - ry high,

hold tight, lean back, get there soon! With my i - ma - gi - na - tion there's no
hold tight, here comes migh - ty me! With my i - ma - gi - na - tion there's no
hold tight, shout my bat - tle - cry! With my i - ma - gi - na - tion there's no

lim - it to the fun, su - per - son - ic roc - ket, my ad -
lim - it to the fun, su - per - tech - no ro - bot, my ad -
lim - it to the fun, su - per - sca - ry mon - ster, my ad -

1. 2.

poco rit.

a tempo

-ven - ture's just be - gun.
-ven - ture's just be - gun.
-ven - ture's just be - gun.

I've

3.

Su - per - sca - ry mon - ster, my ad - ven - ture's just be - gun.

Ready or Not

Words and Music by
Matthew Crossey

With a swing ♩ = 125

(spoken)

One, two, three, four, five, six, sev - en, eight, nine, ten. Rea - dy or not I'm com - ing, rea - dy or not here I come. I'm

27

coun - ting to ten, I hope you've hid - den by then 'cause

To Coda ⊕

rea - dy or not here I come.

1. Are you un - der the stairs?
2. Are you un - der the bed?

(spoken)

NO! Are you next to the chairs?
NO! Is there a coat on your head?

Are you there by the door?
Are you as quiet as can be?

G7 *(spoken)*
C
C/G

NO! Are you crouched on the floor?__
NO! Are you some-where near me?___

1.
C G F²/A G/B

2. *D.S. al Coda*
C G F²/A G/B

CODA
C
C/E

come. I'm

F
C
F
C

coun-ting to ten, I hope you've hid-den by then 'cause

G7
G7/B C N.C.
(spoken)

rea-dy or not here I come. I'VE FOUND YOU!

29

I Love My Car The Best

Words and Music by
Nikki Lewis

With energy ♩ = 100

Lyrics:

1. I love my car the best, it's
(2.) love my train the best, it's
(3.) love my truck the best, it's
(4.) love my plane the best, it's

fast - er than the rest,   it's red and black with
long - er than the rest,   a - round and round the
strong - er than the rest,   it picks things up and
loud - er than the rest,   it swoops and glides a -

Dm⁷   Dm⁷/F   C/G   G⁷   C

shi - ny wheels, I love my car the best.
track it goes, I love my train the best.
puts them down, I love my truck the best.
- cross the sky, I love my plane the best.

G⁷/D   C

Beep, beep,   beep, beep,   beep, beep,
Choo, choo,   choo, choo,   choo, choo,
Vroom, vroom,   vroom, vroom,   vroom, vroom,
Zoom, zoom,   zoom, zoom,   zoom, zoom,

1. 2. 3.   **4.**

G⁷/D   **G⁷/D   N.C.**

beep, beep. 2. I   zoom, zoom.
choo, choo. 3. I
vroom, vroom. 4. I

gliss.

Building Bricks

Words and Music by
Niki Davies

With a swing ♩ = 114

(slower *last time only***)**

1. One brick, two bricks, stead - y as you go.
2. Sev - en bricks, eight bricks, stead - y as you go.
3. Thir - teen, four - teen, stead - y as you go.

Three bricks, four bricks, nice and slow. Five bricks, six bricks, I
Nine bricks, ten bricks, nice and slow. E - lev - en bricks, twelve bricks, I
Fif - teen, six - teen, nice and slow. Sev - en - teen, eight - een, I

think it's get-ting wob - b - ly,_____ is it going to top-ple down?_
think it's get-ting wob - b - ly,_____ is it going to top-ple down?_
think it's get-ting wob - b - ly,___

rit. 2nd time only

(straight quavers)

oh, it's all come tum - bl - ing down!

Mr Jack-In-A-Box

Words and Music by
Mark and Helen Johnson

Moderately ♩ = 144

1. 2. All day long I sit here wait-ing, ho-ping you might pick me up. All day long I

Lyrics:

wish you'd find me, find me soon, 'cause I'm gon-na go POP!

Wind up my han-dle, try to be care-ful,

how ma-ny turns be - fore you wake me up?

Wind up my han-dle, try to be care-ful,

how ma-ny turns be - fore my lit - tle lid goes 'POP'?!

(Boing!)

Say 'hel - lo', I'm pleased to meet you Mis - ter Jack-in - a -

1.

- Box!

2.

- Box!

Say 'hel - lo', I'm pleased to meet you Mis - ter Jack-in - a - Box!

Teddy-Bear Rock

Words and Music by
Ali Dee

With a swing ♩ = 116

Lyrics:

No - bo - dy knows a - bout my ted - dy, no - bo - dy knows what he can do. He does the

Lyrics:

ted - dy - bear stretch,_ he does the

ted - dy - bear flop,_ he does the ted - dy - bear jig,_

he does the ted - dy - bear rock._

Do, do - be - do - wop, the ted - dy - bear rock,

do, do - be - do - wop, the ted - dy - bear rock,

do, do - be - do - wop, my ve - ry, ve - ry spe - cial ted - dy

To Coda ⊕

1.

bear does the ted - dy - bear rock.___

2. *D.%. al Coda*

⊕ **CODA**

39

The Dressing-Up Box

Words and Music by
Nikki Lewis

Steadily ♩ = 114

Lyrics (sung verses):

want to be a prin-cess with a sil-ver crown, I want to be a prin-cess
(2.) want to be a pi-rate with a spot-ty scarf, I want to be a pi-rate
(3.) want to be a dra-gon with sharp and shi-ny claws, I want to be a dra-gon with
(4.) want to be a fire-man with some hea-vy boots, I want to be a fire-man

with a vel-vet gown. I want to be a prin-cess with pink and shi-ny shoes, I
with a yo-ho laugh. I want to be a pi-rate, a patch o-ver my eye, I
green and sli-my jaws. I want to be a dra-gon with a sca-ly chest, I
with a na-vy suit. I want to be a fire-man and slide right down the pole, I

Faster ♩ = 130

G   G/B   C   D7   G   D7

want to be a prin-cess,   a prin-cess   I   will   choose.
want to be a pi - rate,   a   pi - rate   I   will   try.
want to be a dra-gon,   a dra-gon would be   best.
want to be a fire-man,   a fire-man   is   my   goal.

O - pen the box,   the

G   G/B   D7   G   G/B   D7

dress-ing-up box,   I won-der what I could be.   O - pen the box,   the

1. 2. 3.   4.
rit.   a tempo

G   G/B   C   D7   G C/G G   G   D7   G

dress-ing-up box, be a ⎧ prin-cess ⎫ just like   me.
                       ⎪ pi - rate ⎪
                       ⎨ dra - gon ⎬
                       ⎩ fire-man   ⎭

2. I   me.
3. I
4. I

41

Turning The Skipping Rope

Words and Music by
Mary Green and Julie Stanley

Steadily ♩. = 120

F#dim⁷ C/G G G⁷ C C

1. Turn - ing the
2. Turn - ing the

Dm⁷ G⁷ C F C/E

skip - ping rope, one, two, three, in jumps Tho - mas,__
skip - ping rope, one, two, three, in jumps Em - ma,__

D D/F# G C C/E F F#dim⁷

jumps like a flea. Keep on jump - ing while we count:
jumps like a flea. Keep on jump - ing while we count:

One! Two! Three! Four! Five! Six!
One! Two! Three! Four! Five! Six!

Seven! Eight! Time's up Tho-mas,__ you're out.
Seven! Eight! Time's up Em-ma,__ you're out.

Put It Back!

Words and Music by
Mark and Helen Johnson

With a swing ♩ = 124

If you put it down, pick it up, pick it up! If you got it out, put it back!

If you made a mess, clear it up, clear it up! If you got it out, put it back! Don't make some-one else do the dir-ty work,

do what you can do.___ See how quick-ly things can be sort-ed out

1. when we all do what we can, not leave it to a few.

2. leave it to a few.

If you put it down, pick it

up, pick it up! If you got it out, put it back!

If you made a mess, clear it up, clear it up! If you got it out, put it

back! Don't make some-one else do the dir-ty work,

do what you can do.___ See how quick-ly things can be sort-ed out

46

Lyrics:

when we all do what we can, not leave it to a few. If you put it down, pick it

up, pick it up! If you got it out, put it back!

If you made a mess, clear it up, clear it up! If you got it out, put it

back! If you got it out, put it back!

COPYRIGHT & LICENSING

The world of copyright and licensing can seem rather daunting. Whilst it is a legal requirement for schools to comply with copyright law, we recognise that teachers are extremely busy. For this reason we try to make the process of compliance as simple as possible. The guidelines below explain the most common copyright and licensing issues.

Helpful information can be found on the following website:

A Guide to Licensing Copyright in Schools
www.licensing-copyright.org

And remember, we are always happy to help. For advice simply contact our customer services team:
UK: 020 8481 7200   International: +44 20 8481 7200   copyright@outoftheark.com

---

GENERAL GUIDELINES

You are free to use the material in our songbooks for all teaching purposes. However, the reproduction of lyrics and/or music scores (whether for classroom, assembly or collective worship use) and the performance of songs to an audience are both subject to licensing requirements by law. The key points are set out below:

REPRODUCTION OF SONG LYRICS OR MUSICAL SCORES

The following licences from Christian Copyright Licensing Ltd (www.ccli.com) permit photocopying or reproduction of song lyrics and music scores, for example to create song-sheets, overhead transparencies or to display the lyrics or music using any electronic medium.

For UK schools: A Collective Worship Copyright Licence and a Music Reproduction Licence.
For churches: A Church Copyright and Music Reproduction Licence.

The following credit should be included with the lyrics:

'Reproduced by kind permission © Out of the Ark Ltd'

Please ensure that you log the songs that are used on your copy report. (Organisations that do not hold one of the above licences should contact Out of the Ark Music directly for permission.)

A licence IS required by law if you:
• Make photocopies of lyrics
• Create overhead transparencies of lyrics
• Type lyrics into a computer file
• Display lyrics on an interactive whiteboard

PERFORMANCE OF SONGS

If you are performing any of our songs for the public on school premises (i.e. for anybody other than staff and pupils) then royalty payments become due.

Most schools have an arrangement with the Performing Rights Society (PRS) through their local authority. Organisations that do not have such an arrangement should contact Out of the Ark Music directly. The PRS licence does not cover musicals.

Note: If you are staging one of our musicals or nativity plays then a performance licence issued by Out of the Ark Music is required. This licence covers the performance of the songs from the musical.

AUDIO AND VIDEO RECORDINGS

Copying Out of the Ark Music's audio CDs is not permitted without obtaining a licence from the publisher. File-sharing or installation of Out of the Ark Music's audio CD tracks on to a computer are strictly forbidden. If you wish to make an audio or video recording of your performance of any of our works please contact us for further licensing information.